# THE MONASTERY OF KAISARIANI

### Theano Chatzidakis

Dr of history of Byzantine art

APOLLO EDITIONS

The following guides have been published by the APOLLO Editions and can be obtained at the corresponding archaeological sites.

All our books are available in 8 different languages: Greek, English, Spanish, French, Italian, German, Swedish and Japanese.

cover: the southeast side of the church.

© E. Tzaferis, S. A. 52, rue Fokionos Négri - Atenas.

Printed by Grafiche F.G.F. S.p.A. - Milano - Italy
Edition 1980

# INTRODUCTION

The Monastery of Kaisariani, founded in the 11th century A.D. and consecrated to the Presentation of the Virgin in the Temple, is situated on the wooded slope of Mount Hymettos, at a distance of a few miles from the suburb of Kaisariani. A high wall encloses the conventual buildings — the church (katholikon), refectory, bath-house and cells — so that even today the monastery appears well-fortified. In fact, monasteries often served as refuge to the inhabitants of the surrounding areas, when these were threatened by enemy raids or pestilence. The location of Kaisariani,

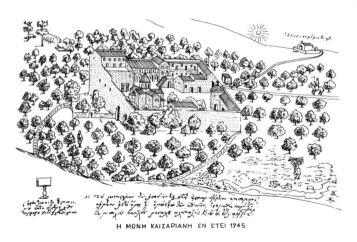

Η ΜΟΝΗ ΚΑΙΣΑΡΙΑΝΗ ΕΝ ΕΤΕΙ 1745.

1. The monk Barsky's sketch of 1745. It shows the Kaisariani monastery buildings and the nearby hill with the church of the Taxiarchs, the monks' cemetery.

3

well-hidden in a ravine of the mountain slope, was best suited for protection. Being invisible from afar, it afforded a view of the whole area, and the possibility of surveying the entire plain as far as the sea and the islands of the Saronic Gulf.

The slope was watered by three springs. The information we have from ancient sources on life in this area is centred on these springs; yet, their identification remains somewhat obscure.

At the east side of the wall, left of the entrance to the monastery, the water of a spring, which earlier historians identified as the ancient Kallia fountain, gushes from a marble ram's head of the Roman period. A little higher, to the southeast of the monastery, there is a shrine, the Hagiasma, which shelters another spring. In older times, the whole population of Athens gathered there to celebrate on Ascension Day.

Tradition has it that on that day a dove flew above the waters of the spring. On the same day, the women participating in the festivity gathered to the northeast of the monastery, around the nearby Kalopoula spring, whose waters were supposed to cure sterility, singing the following song:

"The waters of the Kalopoula are said to have leeches, but they only have beautiful girls."

Some historians have identified the Kalopoula with "Kyllou Pera" — the Hymettian spring known from ancient authors — because its waters were believed to have the same healing properties, and because the names of both springs were thought to be etymologically related.

The slopes of Mount Hymettos are described by the Latin poet Ovid, in the Ars Amatoria. The mountain was also famous for its honey since the time when philosophical schools flourished on its slopes. An anonymous chronicle mentions the schools of Polyzelos and Diodoros. In the 4th century A.D., the bishop Synesios mocked the last Athenian sophists, saying that they were attracting pupils by means of the Hymettian honey rather than through their teaching.

In addition to Kaisariani, a number of monasteries were founded on Mount Hymettos in the Byzantine era and in the years of the Turkish rule: the Moni Asteriou (on the same slope as Kaisariani), the church of St. John Theologue, and the convent of St. John the Hunter (or St. John of the Philosphers).

Although the area of Kaisariani has not yet been systematically investigated, ancient remains reveal the existence of life on this site since the Neolithic age and the 8th century B.C. Most of the

4

remains, however, date from the Classical and, principally, the Roman period. Some of these can be seen today, scattered over the monastery court: a marble stele engraved with the names of priests and other officials of the Eleusinian cult, architraves and capitals carved in relief (such as the one incorrectly placed on the column standing before the entrance to the church). Other pieces have been used as building or decorative material in the katholikon and other parts of the conventual complex (such as the four columns with capitals in the katholikon, and the lintels over the entrance to the narthex and the refectory). Other Roman fragments are built into the walls of the Byzantine church next to the Taxiarchis, on the slope to the southwest of the monastery. Moreover, three late Roman, tile-roofed tombs were discovered in the underground chamber excavated by M. Hadzidakis, near the north side of the katholikon.

The etymology of the monastery's name has been the subject of much discussion. The Turks named the monastery Kots-Bashi, meaning "the ram's head", after the fountain situated left of the entrance. In later times, the monastery was known as Syriani, and it is under this name that it is mentioned in a folk-song:

"A slow walk to Syriani, and honey at Penteli, and the cool water of angels at Daphni".

The earliest written sources on the Monastery of Kaisariani give both names. In 1209, Michael Choniates, Metropolitan of Athens, in a letter addressed to the abbot, calls the monastery "Kaisariani", whereas in 1208, Pope Innocent III refers to the monastery as "Santa Syriani". History students and scholars, mostly of the last century, have expressed a number of varied opinions, all of which have so far remained unconfirmed. According to one theory, the name derives from some Caesars, more precisely the Emperor's brothers exiled to Athens by Irene Athenaea. Another theory ascribes the foundation of the monastery to a certain Caesarius, and still another refers to a woman donor called Syriani. Some suggest that the monastery was named after the founder of a philosophical school on Mount Hymettos, probably called Syrianos. Others support the view that it was named after an icon of the Virgin which must have been brought from Caesaria. Caesarius Daponte (18th century) has also expressed doubts about the origin of the monastery's name. Listing the churches dedicated to the Virgin, he ends as follows:

"The one is called Penteli,
the other is called Kaisariani
— who knows for what reason?"

5

# HISTORY

No written evidence on the monastery is known to us prior to the period of Frankish rule. Apparently, however, the convent was rich and prosperous in the late 12th and early 13th century A.D.

The monks were engaged in apiculture, rearing bees which belonged either to the monastery or to third parties, and the honey produced was one of their chief sources of income. The letter mentioned above, which the Metropolitan Michael Choniates, then living in self-exile on the island of Kea, addressed to the abbot of Kaisariani in 1209, hints at a rather questionable way, whereby the monastery seems to have increased its profits. He writes: "Having reared bees out of his meagre means, the poor abbot of the Monastery of St. John the Baptist gave the beehives to the abbot of Kaisariani to be kept and increased on Mount Hymettos." Four years later, he complained that he had not yet received any income from Kaisariani, whose abbot pretended that the apiary had been destroyed.

In addition to the apiaries, the Monastery of Kaisariani possessed estates and dependencies on Mt. Hymettos and in other parts of Attica (Anavyssos), and must have played an important role in the surrounding area and the city of Athens. It also appears that the abbots of the monastery were able to come to terms with the successive foreign conquerors, in order to secure certain privileges for their convent. In effect, when Athens was deserted after the Frankish conquest of 1204, Pope Innocent III placed the monasteries on Mount Hymettos, including Kaisariani, under the jurisdiction of the Latin Archibishop of Athens. But the abbot of Kaisariani wasted no time in declaring submission to the Pope himself, so that the monastery retained its freedom and privilege of tax immunity. When the Turks occupied Attica in 1458, and Mehmed II came to Athens, he was received by the abbot of Kaisariani, who delivered up to him the keys of the city, as we are told by an unconfirmed legend contained in the writings of the traveller Spon (1675). As a result, the Sultan exempted the monastery of Kaisariani from taxation, limiting its obligations to the annual payment of a token sum of insignificant value (one tsekin). The monastery was granted similar exemption from taxation, not only by the Franks and Turks, but also by the Greek Patriarchate.

A sigil issued in 1678 by Patriarch Dionysios IV confirms older Frankish documents and earlier patriarchal decrees of the first years of the Turkish rule, recognising the monastery as stavropegiaki, i.e. "free and immune from taxation", for its own property towards the Metropolitan of Athens, to whom it has only one obligation — namely, to commemorate him in the liturgy. After the siege of Athens and its temporary occupation by Morosini's Venetain troops in 1687, Attica was deserted as the population fled to the Peloponnese in order to escape persecutions, raids and pestilence. At that time, the revenues of the Metropolis were extremely meagre and insufficient. In the early 18th century, when the country was re-inhabited, Patriarch Jeremiah III isssued a sigil (1716) annulling the privileges of several monasteries of the stavropegiaki type, including that of Kaisariani, which then became a parochial convent under the Metropolis of Athens. The Patriarch vindicated his decision as follows: "Because holy monasteries of the stavropegiaki type, such as the so-called Monastery of Kaisariani, whose protection-enjoying abbots have little by little turned the patriarchal privilege and freedom accorded to them to their own advantage and power, have inappropriately deviated from the right way."

It is not known how long the Patriarch's decision remained in force. In any event, in 1778, the monastery enjoyed again its old privileges, which it preserved until 1790. At that time, the abbots of other Hymettian monasteries, together with the notables and elders of Athens, claiming that Kaisariani was in heavy debt due to bad administration and fearing that this would cause the fall of the monastery into the hands of the Turkish ruler Hadji Ali Haseki, "begged the Metropolitan of Athens to take in his own hands the helm of this sinking ship", as expressed in their letter. In 1792, a sigil issued by Patriarch Neophytos abolished the independence of the monastery and placed it again under the Metropolitan of Athens. This decision rescued the monastery from the Turkish ruler, but failed to prevent its decline and final collapse. A document of the city elders describes the state of the monastery in 1824: "… and it thus began to lose its independence and be administered as private property of the holy high priests. But what happened to it and what was its fate? The convent that could save and enlighten many human souls now became the abode of animals, oxen, donkeys and horses. The precious parchment namuscripts of the library were sold to the English and the rest were used by the cooks of the Metropolis." During the siege of Athens by the Turks, the library of the monastery, together with that of the Metropolis, was transported to the Acropolis and the books were used to ignite cartridges. In King

Otto's time, Kaisariani became a monastery for nuns.

In its age of prosperity, the monastery was a cultural centre for the whole region. It had a rich library, and its abbots were scholars and renowned teachers at the schools of Athens. the names of Theophanis and Ioannis Doryanos appear in a monastery codex dating from 1556. In 1572, Sophronios Stanitsas renovated the conventual dependency of St. John the Baptist, where an inscription records the name of Gregorios Gemistos. Iezekiel Stephakis, who was abbot of the monastery in 1675, is described by the travellers Spon and Wheler as a scholar of Greek literature and history as well as a Platonic philosopher. An inscription on the narthex of the church tells us that Paisios Boulismas and the "most learned" Abbot Hierotheos lived in 1682 at Kaisariani. Theophanis Kaballaris taught (1722-28) "literary and scientific subjects" to the youths who attended the school founded by Gregorios Sotiris at Athens; later he served as abbot of Kaisariani, where he stayed to his last days (shortly after 1782).

The leading nobility of Athens was also associated with the Monastery of Kaisariani. The Benizeloi, one of the greatest Athenian families whose members remained powerful and influential throughout the entire period of the Turkish rule, the Misseraliotai, and other notable families owned estates on Mount Hymettos. The remains of the towers they built to supervise these estates are still visible on this mountain slope. The Benizeloi even had such a tower — known to this day as the "tower of Benizelos" — within the monastery itself. It is there that the "noble and scholarly" Benizelos, son of Ioannis Benizelos, sought refuge with his mother and sisters in 1682, when Athens was ravaged by an epidemic. Wishing to decorate the monastery, he commissioned Ioannis Hypatos to paint the walls of the narthex. The monastery was also associated with Panagiotis, son of Alexandros, Soterianos. His grave (1789), found near the entrance to the narthex, bore a marble stele which is now at the Byzantine Museum in Athens.

## THE MONUMENTS

### The earliest group of buildings.

We have no documentary evidence for Kaisariani in the early Christian period, or indeed until the time of the Frankish conquest. It would appear from the surviving remains that the first Christian

8

establishment was founded on the hill which rises a short distance south west of the present monastery. This is probably the site to which Michael Honiatis is referring when he extols the view from Hymettos over Attica to the islands of the Saronic Gulf, Psittalia, Salamis and Aigina.

On this hill to-day stand the later church of the Taxiarchs (St Michael and St Gabriel), which was used by the monks as a burial place, and the remains of a Byzantine church, beside which is the ruined church of St Mark, which must have been built during the Frankish occupation. The 1958 excavations of M. Hadzidakis behind the sanctuary apses of the Byzantine church revealed the foundations of a 5th - 6th century Early Christian basilica, with three aisles and three semicircular apses. The marble elements from this basilica, the reliefs and panels of the iconostasis, were later used to embellish the Kaisariani church. They can be seen in the restored iconostasis of the main church, while other fragments serve as ornamental lintels. or are incorporated in the exterior west wall of the narthex.

A church was built on the same spot as the Early Christian basilica, perhaps of the Taxiarchs, and probably about the 10th century, in other words before the church of the Blessed Virgin. To-day it is preserved to a very low height, except for the south apse. the church has three semi-hexagonal apses, and the breadth of the nave is greater than that of the transepts, which would have caused the dome spanning their intersection to be elliptical in plan. The west corner bays are smaller than the east ones, and are divided from the central nave by blank walls. These features place it close to the transitional type of Greek church that spread through Greece during the 10th - 9th centuries, and in which builders were developing and perfecting the domed cross-in-square form of church.

Skripou church is the best known example of this type, but the church beside the Taxiarchs', while smaller in size, represents a stage nearer the mature cruciform style. At all events the massive side-walls of the arms of the cross are still being employed to support the weight of the dome, and the transverse arms of the cross terminate externally in projecting arches.

The construction of the walls, with large unworked stones and bricks, not laid in regular courses, and the incorporation of Roman architraves and other fragments, are further indication that the church should be dated earlier than the 11th century.

Alongside this Byzantine church and against its south wall was built, some time after the Frankish conquest, a single-aisled church, rectangular, with vaulted roof and semi-hexagonal apse, which to-day is largely in ruins. It was dedicated to St Mark and must have been a Catholic church, a probability further strengthened by the name Frankomonasteri given to the locality in later years. By then, however, the monastic centre had already been moved to the less exposed position where it is to-day.

## The Byzantine Monastery.

The Kaisariani monastery was built in the 11th century on top of the foundations of an ancient secular building of unknown period. Traces of it are visible behind the sanctuary of the church and extend eastwards as far as the enclosure wall.

Apart from the main church and the bath-house, which are original 11th century structures, the narthex, bell-tower and the side-chapel of St Anthony are later additions belonging to the time of

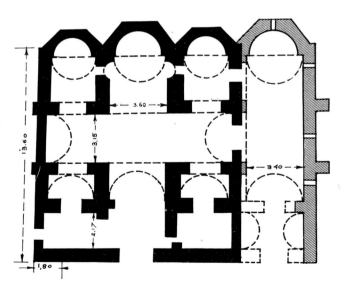

2. View of the Byzantine and Frankish churches on the hill of the Taxiarchs.

the Turkish occupation.

The sketch by the itinerant monk Barskji gives a graphic picture of the condition of the buildings when he visited them in 1745.

The Monastery, which is surrounded by a wall, has two entrances: the main one on the west and a smaller one on the east. The buildings are set around a courtyard: on the east side the church; on the west the refectory and kitchen; on the south the bath-house, converted into the monastery olive-press in Turkish times; and beside it miscellaneous buildings, including the monks' cells opening onto a gallery. Roughly in the centre of this wing stands the Tower of Benizelos, a square structure with an external stairway built against the facade.

# THE CHURCH

### Architecture.

The church, concrated to the Presentation of the Virgin, belongs to the inscribed cruciform composite Greek type (M. Soteriou), or alternatively to the semi-composite tetrakionion type (A. Orlandos). The main church has a square plan in which are inscribed the arms of the cross. The sanctuary apses are joined to the church without any intervening bays. Four columns from an ancient temple support the dome, the weight of which is also carried on the four barrel vaults roofing the arms of the cross. The side bays are roofed by smaller vaults, the eastern ones covering the parabemata, while the sanctuary itself is covered by the vault over the eastern arm of the cross. Thus the interior of the church comprises a single entity with symmetrically roofed spaces, and the arrangement and roofing of the sanctuary are not differentiated structurally from the rest of the church. Level with the bottom of the vaulting runs a moulded cornice bearing murals. The church of Panayia Gorgoepikoos in Athens is of the same type, and certain churches in the Mani (Ayios Yiannis, Keria), in Messenia and in Locris (the Taxiarch). What characterises Kaisariani and other churches of the 11th century, are the proportions: the narrow side-bays, and the dome with its very tall drum, pierced by eight windows, accentuate the feeling of loftiness within the interior of the church.

The organisation of the interior space is clearly discernible from the outside. The elevated cruciform design stands out above the lower corner bays, and the conches of the sanctuary are laid out in semi-hexagonal apses. The simple volumes rise cleanly upwards to create a single harmonious whole. All the walling, of pure Greek

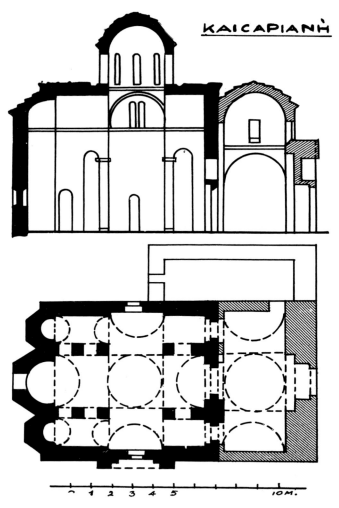

**KAICAPIANH**

3. View of the church.

style, follows the stone with brick surround system, in which regular courses of stone alternate with rows of bricks, uninterrupted by decorative bands; it is exemplified to perfection in the construction of the sanctuary apses. The central apse is embellished with a massively decorated double window, which is surmounted by an arch of tiles and framed by a pattern of tiling that follows the curves of the two window arches. The tiles framing the window in the north apse have the same pattern.

The octagonal dome with its straght cornice has a single window in each of its sides; it is decorated in the same austere fashion with two rows of tiles, and a straght saw-tooth band emphsises the simpliciy of the ornamentation. In this respect Kaisariani contrasts with most of the Athens churches of the period, in which the cupola windows are bordered by engaged pillars and topped by arches, in such a way that the lower edge of the cupola is contoured to the curves of the window arches.

The original entrance was directly through the west wall without any intermediate narthex; this is apparent from the decoration of the entrances, with their marble thresholds and lintels and their arched openings.

There is another entrance on the north side; it has a marble threshold and a Roman lintel, and is surmounted by a projecting arch over all the end wall of the north transept, which is pierced by a double window. This style of construction is often seen in the side elevations of 11th century churches in Athens (Moni Petraki, Sotira Lykodimou) and elsewhere (Osios Loukas, Dafni). On a level with the architrave and above the projecting arch traces can be detected which may have belonged to arch supports. It is probable that on this side of the church some sort of pronaos or porch was built to protect the north entrance. Whether or not this was so, the particularly careful construction on this side of the church indicates that it had some special importance. Under the north courtyard an underground vaulted chamber was found, which communicates with the church and once served as an ossuary.

The narthex, which was added in Turkish times, and certainly not later than 1682, has a barrel vault with central cupola and drum.

**Mural Paintings.**

No trace remains of the original decoration in the church. The oldest mural is to be found on the ouside of the south wall of the church, which is to-day within the sanctuary of the side-chapel of St

Anthony. It depicts Our Lady facing towards the left, in prayer, and is the remains of a Deesis; the profusion of lines in the drawing denotes a provincial style of the 14th century. The murals within the church and narthex date to the time of the Turkish occupation. In the main church murals cover the cupola, the drum of the cupola, the sanctuary apse, and all the upper surfaces including the end walls and cornices of the vaults which mark out the four arms of the cross. The arrangement of the paintings follows the established scheme. Christ Pantocrator is in the cupola. On the upper part of the drum, which is divided into two zones, are the Preparation of the Throne, the Blessed Virgin, John the Baptist, angels and the tetramorph (a composition including the symbols of the four Evangelists); on the lower part, between the windows, are the prophets, and in the four pendentives, the Evangelists.

In the conch of the apse is the Virgin Platytera enthroned, and flanked by adoring angels. On the frieze underneath is the Divine Liturgy, and below that the Communion of the Apostles. In the lowest zone are the co-officiating Fathers John Chrysostomos, Basil, Gregory and Athanasios.

On the vaulting of the four arms of the cross and the end wall of the west arm scenes of the Christ Cycle are portrayed. Starting on the south side of the eastern vault, which roofs the sanctuary, the iconographic cycle follows the series of events in the life of Christ: the Nativity, Presentation, Baptism, Transfiguration, Raising of Lazarus, Entry into Jerusalem, Last Supper, Resurrection, Incredulity of Thomas, Ascension and the Day of Pentecost. The scenes of the Crucifixion, Annunciation and Assumption are missing. On the south wall of the south transept is the Baptist in Jordan; on the north wall of the north transept are to the left of the window the Holy Women at the Empty Tomb, and on the right the Sleeping Sentries.

A broad band with prophets against a background of ornamental sprays and leaves, running along the top of the vaulting, separates, the scenes on either side of each arm.

The wall paintings are not remarkable for their innovation in terms of iconographic types or treatment of forms. The balanced compositions and the harmonious disposition of figures within the alloted field conform to 16th century Cretan models such as are found in the churches of Mt Athos, and which the Kaisariani painter has imitated with considerable fidelity. The representations of the Christ Cycle (the Twelve Feasts of Christ) follow these models not

14

4. 14th century mural in the side-shapel of St Antomy.

only in general composition but also in the treatment of detail; look, for example, at the personification of the river Jordan in the Baptism, the buildings in the Presentation, or the posture of the apostles in the Last Supper. At the same time the painter draws on later models, derived from the portable Cretan ikons, as exemplified in the type of the Virgin Platytera, seated on a marble throne and surrounded by prophets, the work of Emmnuel Tzane (1664). A similar return to the Cretan style of the 16th century is noticeable in the figures, but with a certain difference. The majority of the paintings, like those in the vault over the sanctuary, for example the Nativity, Pentecost, Presentation and Ascension, are notable for their assured drawing, quiet movement, the plasticity of their cleanly delineated figures and their austere harmony of colour. On the other hand the Transfiguration, Raising of Lazarus and Resurrection are marked by a carelessness both in draughtsmanship and the use of colour. In contrast with other scenes, certain details such as the rendering of the small figure on top of the gate in the Incredulity of Thomas and the composition of the sleeping soldiers in the scene of the Holy Women at the Tomb, and particularly the relief deisgn on the shield and shoulder-plate, show familiarity with the freer, more expressive style that grew up under western influences. Also characteristic, although outside of the Cretan tradition, are the liturgical vestments with embroidered sprays worn by the prophets and angels in the drum of the dome, and in the Divine Liturgy, which are reproductions of Turkish fabrics of the period.

The conservative character of the Kaisariani murals led earlier students to believe that they had been painted in the 16th century, certainly earlier than the narthex. Recent studies, however, have shown that this tendency to return to earlier models which gives the painting a certain academic quality, together with the use of later models such as the portable Cretan ikons and particularly Emmanuel Tzane, and the presence of elements bearing the stamp of western influence, are a general characteristic of the early 18th century.

The mural paintings in the main church must have been executed by a painter operating in just such a climate, who was a skilled and careful craftsman with distinctly conservative tendencies, very much in keeping with a period in which Attica was starting to be repopulated by its inhabitants, who had fled to the Peloponnese at the time of the Venetian conquest. It was at this time that the artistic influence of an Argive painter, George Markos, was predominant in the churches of Attica and the wall paintings at Kaisariani were not uninfluenced by his work. Some further confirmation of this is suggested by the fact that among Markos' assistants — in the church of the Assumption at Koropi and the-Faneromeni on Salamis— we find the name of Nikolaos Benizelos, son of the Benizelos who was closely associated with the monastery and so concerned in the decoration of its church.


## Narthex.

Kaisariani monastery was consecrated to the Presentation of the Virgin, and this scene is found repeated twice in the narthex: on the outside west wall within the arch surmounting the entrance into the narthex, and on the inside, above the left hand pilaster of the central door from the narthex into the main church. Over the right hand pilaster is the Ascension. On the west wall directly over the entrance an inscription recounts the names and circumstances of the people who contributed to the painting of the murals:

"This pronaos or narthex has been decorated at the expense of those who sought refuge in the monastery for fear of the plague, through the mighty hand of the All-praised Trinity and the protection of the Blessed Virgin; they being the noble and learned Benizelos, son of John, together with his noble sisters and mother and all the rest of his retinue; in the term of the most learned monk, the abbot Hierotheos; by the hand of John Hypatos of the Peloponnese. The year 1682 on the 20th day of August."

The symbolic portrayal of the Holy Trinity in the cupola is no doubt linked with its mention in the inscription. On the drum of the dome there are two bands, as in the main church: on the upper, the Preparation of the Throne, the Virgin, John the Baptist and the angels; on the lower, full length prophets. The hymnographers Kosmas, Joseph and John the Damascene are in the pendentives, but the fourth has been destroyed.

Over the inscription on the west wall is a rare iconographic representation of the Tabernacle of the Witness, with the twelve tribes of Israel offering gifts while Moses and Aaron sacrifice before the Lord's Table.

The scenes decorating the roof and walls of the vaults are divided into rectangular panels surrounded by a frame, and in the zone beneath are depicted the figures of ascetics and saints.

The south vault of the narthex is occupied by scenes from the parables: the Publican and the Pharisee, the Prodigal Son, and the Good Samaritan on the east; the Rich Fool, the Wicked Husbandmen, the Sower, and the Rich Man and Lazarus on the west.

On the east side of the north vault are four scenes from the book of James: the Presentation of the Doves in the Temple, the Annunciation to Joachim and Anna, the Birth of the Virgin, and the Virgin Mary Blessed by the Priests. On the west wall of the vault are four scenes from the Morning gospels: Peter and John at the Empty Tomb the Journey to Emmaus, the "Touch Me Not", and the Appearance of Christ to the Disciples at Lake Tiberius.

On the end walls of the vaults are two complementary representations: on the north wall the Tree of Jesse, or the genealogical tree of the Virgin, in which the descendants of Jesse are depicted on branches growing out of his body. On the south wall is the Spiritual Posterity of Christ, according to the gospel of St John: "I am the vine and ye are the branches." Christ is shown on the trunk of a vine while the twelve apostles appear among the branches.

The iconographic arrangement of the murals in the narthex conforms to the function and subject matter of the scenes portrayed (the Presentation, scenes from the Birth of the Blessed Virgin, the Holy Trinity), but in some of the representations of the parables, such as the Rich Fool, the Rich Man and Lazarus, or the Wicked Husbandmen, we may perhaps detect references to the noble donor Benizelos and the management of his properties.

A blend of influences is apparent in the pictures, that often diverges from the canons of 16th century ikon painting. The Tabernacle of the Witness and the Pharisee and the Publican were inspired by more sophisticated models, in which human figures are numerous; indeed all the parable scenes are of this type. The requirements of narrative caused the painter, John Hypatos, to give a detailed rendering of the traditional episodes, which are crowded and compressed within the set limits of the picture.. The graphic details within each scene illustrate the directness of his art: the labourers emptying sacks of food, the carpenters cutting wood, and the wounded man "who fell among thieves" being taken to the inn bundled up on a donkey.

The painter's simple, profuse brushwork clearly delineates the figures and renders schematically the folds of the drapery and parts of the human body. This is particularly apparent in the nudes in the

Good Samaritan, which are reminiscent of shadow theatre figures, while in the persons of the two shepherds in the Annunciation to Joachim and Anna an attempt is made to display grace and neatness.

The murals are painted on a black background, with the result that the colour contrasts and the masses of the forms are made to stand out; the ground usually has a stipple decoration. However in the treatment of the bare parts of the body and the faces there is very little use of tonal gradation, and none at all in some places. The sparing use of white serves to lighten the masses and give modelling to the flesh, which with its dark olive undertone gives the impression, enhanced by the worn condition of the painting, that all the people are swarthy.

John Hypatos has a special sense of colour, which preserves its earthy tones even when these have little correspondence with reality. Mountains or buildings form a setting that has no relation with the world of actuality. According to the requirements of the composition in terms of balance mountains may be painted terracotta, grey and red with black shadows, as in the Good Samaritan, or red with broad white stripes, as in the Prodigal Son.

All the general characteristics of 17th century Greek mural painting are present in the decoration of the Kaisariani narthex. What is sometimes called the folk stream of art makes itself apparent in the simplicity of the elements of composition and the treatment of forms. It exhibits an anti-classical tendency which is a far cry from the styles so familiar in the monasteries of Mt Athos. In fact by the 17th century Cretan painters are no longer found on the mainland of Greece, and most of the artists of the period come from the Peloponnese, and especially Nauplion, such as the Moschos brothers and Kakavas. John Hypatos, with his Kaisariani murals, belongs to this class of Peloponnesian painters who, as Fotis Kontoglou says, "possess a curious quality of archaism that is not just a dead and distant memory of the classical world, but a living element springing from deep down in the spirit of the people."

**The Bath-house.**

The trefoil building on the left of the eastern entrance, facing the south side of the church, and built around a natural spring, belongs with the 11th century monastery. It is roofed by a hemispherical cupola, without a drum, which is supported on four pendentives. The cupola has eight windows which, with four others in the walls, give light to the interior. The building is contemporary with the main church and has the same system of regular courses with alternating squared stones and bricks. Fragments of pottery found in the course of the restoration date to the same period. During the Turkish occupation it was incorporaed into a massive structure that served as the Monastery oil press. Alterations and additions had so changed the appearance of the building that its original function was a matter of speculation. At one time it was thought to be a Holy Spring because traces of a water conduit were found on the inside. Later hot air ducts and square hypocaust pillars were discovered, features indicating that the building had originally been the monastery bath-house. The Kaisariani bath-house, along with similar ones preserved at Dafni and the Monastery of Zoodohos Piyi at Dervenosalesi on Mt Kitheron, are among the very few examples known from the period, and they are witness to the monastic rule which specified the frequent practice of ablutions. The method of

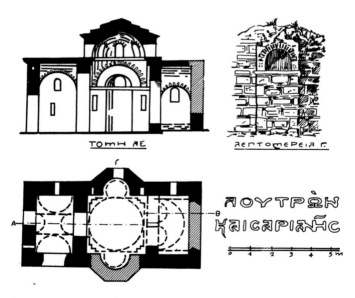

ΤΟΜΗ ΑΕ

ΛΕΠΤΟΜΕΡΕΙΑ Γ

ΛΟΥΤΡΩΝ
ΚΑΙΣΑΡΙΑΝΗC

5. View of the refectory and kitchen.

construction is a continuation from the tradition of Roman baths, and it was later to be adopted in the building of Turkish baths. The Zoodohos Piyi bath-house had built benches in the main chamber. At Kaisariani marble benches can be seen in the courtyard arranged in a ring about a circular marble basin.

**Refectory.**

The refectory and kitchen are housed together in a single building by the western enclosure wall, opposite the front of the church. The refectory is a long rectangular, vaulted hall divided into two parts. The entrance chamber, in between the kitchen and the main hall, served as a storeroom for victuals, as is shown by the large storage jars that were found there still in place. The main hall has three blind apses along the east and west walls; the three eastern ones have windows. At the north end an apse is inscribed in the

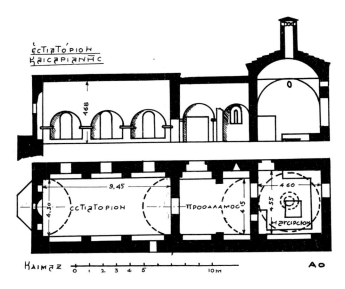

6. View of the bath-house.

thickness of the wall, which on the outside is straight; this was reserved for the abbots's place. The kitchen, built against the south end of the refectory, is square and has a cupola, out of which rises the chimney. The fireplace is in the centre, and around it stone benches are built along the four walls.

# BIBLIOGRAPHY

Akominatos, Michael. the Preserved Works, ed. Sp. Lambrou. Athens 1880, vol II p 131 (Greek text).

Spon, J. Voyage en Grèce. 1678, vol I, p 331.

Gregorovius. Istoria tis poleos Athinon, metafr. Sp. Lambrou. Athens 1904, vols I and II.

Kambouroglou, D. Istoria ton Athinaion. Athens 1889.

Kambouroglou, D. Mnimia tis istorias ton Athinaion. Athens 1891.

Kambouroglou, D. Anadromaris tis Attikis. Athens 1914.

Kambouroglou, D. Athinaikon arhondoloyion. Athens 1921.

Filadelfevs, Th. Istoria ton Athinon epi tourkokratias. Athens 1902

Strygowski, I. Kaisariani, metafr. Sp. Lambrou. Arch. Eph. 1902, pp 53-95.

Hamilton, J.A. The Church of Kaissariani in Attica. Aberdeen 1916.

Millet, G. L'Ecole greque dans l'architecture byzantine. Paris 1916.

Tsima-Papahadzidakis, Xyngopoulos, Kondoglou. Tihografia ekklision Ymittou, Monai Theologou kai Kaisarianis. ed. AE Ellinikes Tehnes. Athens 1933.

Xyngopolos, A. Shediasma istorias tis thriskevtikis zografikis meta tin alosin. Athens 1957.

Orlandos, A. I Ayia Trias Kriezoti. AVME vol v, 1939-40, pp 7-8.

Orlandos, A. Evretirion ton mesaionikon mnimion Ellados, Mnimia Attikis. Athens 1927, vol I, no 3, pp 158 - 164.

Orlandos, A. Monastiriaki arhtektoniki. Athens 1958.

Papayianopolos Palaios, A. Kaisariani. Athens 1940

Sotiriou, M. Loutrones kai ayiasmata en Attiki. Praktika HAE 1934-5, pp 85 - 92.

Sotiriou, M. O Naos tis Skripous Viotias. Arch. Eph. 1931, p i35.

Sotiriou, M. To katholikon tis monis Petraki. DHAE, per. 4, vol II, 1960-61, p 136.

Hadzidakis, M. Skafikai erevnai en ti moni Kaisariani. PAE 1949, pp 44 - 50;

1950, pp 138-144.

Hadzidakis, M. Constribution à l'étude de la peinture postbyzantine. Offprint from Hellénism Contemporain, May 1953

Hadzidakis, M. Vizantini Athina. Athens 1956, figs 99-120.

Hadzidakis, M. Arch. Delt. 16 (1960), Hronika, p 66, pl 53b.

ILLUSTRATIONS

The first Christian centre at Kaisariani with the ruins of the Early
Christian basilica and 10th cent. Byzantine church, and the
Frankish church of St Mark on the right.

The front of the 11th cent. church with the later narthex and the side-chapel of St Antony.

Particular care was given to the construction of the north transept
of the church: the entrance, with Roman lintel and projecting
arch spanning the north face, with its double window.

The sanctuary apse seen from above the screen, with the 18th cent. murals:
the Virgin Platytera (a copy of the picture by Emmanuel Tzane), with the
Holy Liturgy below, and the Communion of the Apostles below that.

On the lowest zone of the sanctuary apse are the church fathers:
visible here are St Athanasius and St John.

The church screen is made up of fragments belonging to the
Early Christian basilica. The cupola rests on ancient columns
with capitals.

The cupola with the Pantocrator and the Preparation of the
Throne; the prophets can just be made out between the
windows.

The vaults are decorated with scenes from the Christ Cycle: on the left, the sanctuary vault with the Birth and Presentation; on the right, the south vault with the Baptism.

The Births, in the sanctuary vault.

The Presentation, in the sanctuary vault.

the Baptism, in the south transept.

The Last Supper, in the nave.

In the narthex, the pilaster to the right of the central doorway
into the main church is painted with the Ascension.

The narthex murals were executed by the Peloponnesian painter John Hypatos in 1682 at the expense of the nobleman Benizelos, who had taken refuge at Kaisariani with his family to escape the plague. This is the account given in the dedicatory inscription below the scene of the Tabernacle of the Witness on the west wall, over the entrance into the narthex.

The parable of the Good Samaritan, in the south vault of the narthex.

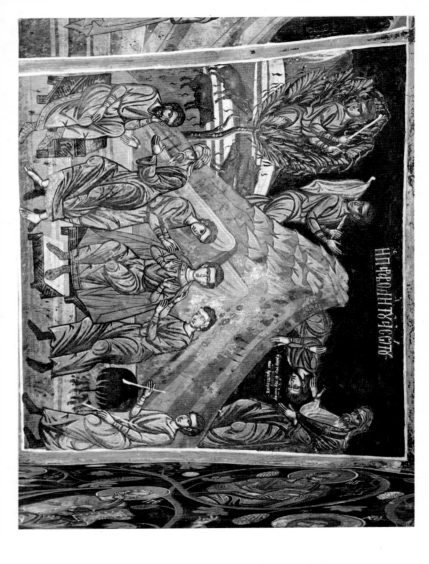

The parable of the Prodigal Son, in the south vault of the narthex.

The parable of the Pharisee and the Publican, in the same vault.

The Prayer of Joachim and Anna from the Book of James, in the
north vault of the narthex.

A scene from the Morning gospels, in the north vault of the
narthex: the Holy Women at the Tomb, and the "Touch me
Not."

Interior of the courtyard at Kaisariani, with the eastern entrance and the 11th cent. bath-house on the right.

The refectory and kitchen with its high chimney are buildings
of the Turkish period, and are on the west side of the court,
facing the church.

Later buildings on the east, including the marble entrance to the olive press and the stairway to the cells.

Various buildings, including the monks' cells and Benizelos'
Tower in the centre, on the south side of the court.